The Obvious Flap

THE OBVIOUS FLAP

GARY BARWIN
& GREGORY BETTS

BOOKTHUG \ TORONTO, 2011

The production of this book was made possible through the generous
assistance of the Canada Council for the Arts and the Ontario Arts Council.

 Canada Council **Conseil des Arts**
for the Arts **du Canada**

 **ONTARIO ARTS COUNCIL**
CONSEIL DES ARTS DE L'ONTARIO

Printed in Canada.

Library and Archives Canada Cataloguing in Publication

Barwin, Gary
    The obvious flap / Gary Barwin, Gregory Betts.

Poems.
ISBN 978-1-897388-78-5

    I. Betts, Gregory, 1975- II. Title.

PS8553.A783O28 2011   C811'.54   C2011-901539-0

take it away

CONTENTS

DEADWOOD

i don't know

I don't know, I admit that as a grammatical parallel, a residue

would in fact be more resonant in its new bed of semantic

noise. On the bus are the things I will have as a referent outside

the sentence. Is it possible to think of this as some kind of narrative

(at least to me) emerged, one that excluded me if I had just one accordion

if I had a child I was an ant farm a pickle trainer a philosophy of clowning

auditor my resume a maraschino cherry that fits on my nose

and covered by ants breathe the instructors say sit in class

and breathe smoke fills the room I am singing here let me light

your birthday candles I have lungs like desert islands on one

of them a guy in an inner tube praying to be puzzled as I wrote.

I don't know, I admit that as a grammatical parallel, a residue

would in fact be more resonant in its new bed of semantic

noise. On the bus are the things I will have as a referent outside

the sentence. Is it possible to think of this as some kind of narrative

(at least to me) emerged, one that excluded me if I had just one accordion

if I had a child I was an ant farm a pickle trainer a philosophy of clowning

auditor my resume a maraschino cherry that fits on my nose

and covered by ants breathe the instructors say sit in class

and breathe smoke fills the room I am singing here let me light

your birthday candles I have lungs like desert islands on one

of them a guy in an inner tube praying to be puzzled as I wrote.

no   , I   am   a residue

noise   the things I   have

     I   think of   as

         one hat   one accordion

     an ant   a pickle   a   clown

  my   hat fits on my nose

and   ant   in class

    fills the room   let me

     have   land

   in an inner   puzzle   as I   rot

note, I, I   am   a residue

                                        of semantic

noise   the things I   have

          I   think of   as

          one hat   one accordion

an not   a pistle   &   clown

my   hat fits on my nose

and   ant   in class

          fills the room   let me

               have   land

     in an inner   puzzle as I rot

SIMILINES I

1.

the soft would
of lumber

the a of b
the 1 of 2
the me of you

2.

the windows' trust
the sleeping door

the air of
definite fire

braiding smoke
with 1 or 2
of my fingers
angles linger
grammar of augury of

*

like really

you don't know
the half of it

you mean 'i'?

3.

the soft should
of literature

like

standing on the
North Pole
trying
to walk East

instead

polar bears,
French fedoras,
misfits called
Degolas

4.

stars like stars
pewter like pewter
wings like wings

punch like punch
circle like circle
feast like feast

rose like
Laura like
St. George
like Spadina

5.

Beatrice
beat
Beatrice
beat rice
Beatrice
bat ice
  try
be at i
be at i
be at i

6.

not everyone is a poet
my dog for instance
is a flower
or a hedge

like

from the pole
look south
or else north

7.

what does my dog look like?
look, what does my dog like?
like, look what my dog does
does my dog like what look?
does like my dog

8.

like
perhaps by calling a poem
a poem it becomes
a dog

here, poem
sit
stay
good poem

9.

Beatrice,
i've tried bat ice
i've tried to be at
1
with myself
to have a positive
beatitude

but like
beat it
like
beat

punch

10.

i'm rolling in
half of it

the other half of it
i'm rolling in is
rolling in i

11.

i look like
the dog like dogs
the pewter pewters
the wings of stars
like star wings
St. George or Laura
Spadina
Spadina
Beatrice punch
a circle circles
a feast of poles
walking north in all directions

instead
a polar bear in a fedora
the infinite hat brim surrounding
the dog that is poem

i trust only windows

lie down
play dead
sleep

only windows

CHORA SEA

I.

I am not chora, I don't want chora. Here in hedra, there is the movement between the chora, like the lisp of seas beneath continents. I rush from song to the next, holding my breath.

I'm not choral, keep my hedra below the clouds, space up my sleeve. In this place, gravity dims, Pangea words begin to separate from my meaning.

> some kind of matrix
> some kind of space
> some kind
>
> time
>
> you go bowling?
> yes
> i go bowling with Apollo
> a pair of guise
> apologize

is that a first growth forest
or are you just happy
to be me?

my bowling eyes rolling

gutterball in the great beyonder:

paradise

what if the rain
referred to something else?
and bowling
and shoes
were done with the mouth?

my god
is my god

     Geronimo

the space of dancing
dionancing
sing

like Celine

(line?)

in

          you make the lung road

          i take the short breath

are you
happy to see me
to see you
happy?

i love

you like

an elephant

O O O O that shaking
takes us
Bacchus

       alive alive O

off the grid & grinning

grid-ironing the empty air
removing space/time wrinkles
& the smooth brain

rolling down the lane

seen change:

iron and gridstone brimming
with shoes
possibility
larynxes

irony and brimstone grinning
with issues
passability
Loraxes

i wouldn't be a member of any language
that would have i

i love

you like

irrelevant

and in Bacchus' fields
poppies O
beneath Apollo
stones and crows

in back field
imbeciles sit oned
feet plopped in glass ponds
held in escrow

they are happy
to tell stories
of languages and myths
that surround you

they sing a tear to your i
many open mouths

    O O O O

    choiral

    hedra and shoulders above the rest

    the i of your ipple

    and bininis for you

                    they are a chorus

                     (line?)

                    between you
                    and your other
                    happiness

"my other line is an iambic"

in chora
  we (subject)
    enter the din
    nether (grammar) nor
  flash (punctation/ black planet
relaxe (verb)

beneath the earth's surface
someone restarts the sentence with
heart paddles

a river
                    the trees

horizon (line) _____

                    river rising

horizon (line) _____

our eyes on
(riverizon)
line?

i don't know

      a journal of river
      trees, paddles
      din

what is that on the horizon?
the horizon

      pulling clouds
      like teeth

over an elephant
hope is
a trunk in the fog

hundreds of clowns climb out
of the lungs
history jumps into a pool
we close our eyes

i love

you like

an alphabet

cloudbumpers
words
fogmechanicals

one s eye
found an
emoticon to represent
emoticons

sigh

words like/words
words

her eyes on
her rising

cloud   rain   cloud

                tree

a fog of throat
fingers cloud
a flag of words

                    i rest
                    continent

that's the idea
now we're somewhere
once again

or just to the
north of it

II.

The influence of something with something else on the surface of
an event remain cloaked in the dim here. And the stores of poppies
in your mouth. Meanwhile, rain flashes beneath clouds, and still you
speak of the words and the poppies of your sentence. There was a you,
and you came to the development of one sweet sum which expresses
itself as a bursting forth flame in the shanty your voice telling of them.

O burnished blackwing! If haply you seek your image in the delved
brain's wax museum, you'll find only that which contains a nether
cloud to your perfect matrix. But what of the material of the idea of
a gerund along with the possibility of being both here and lost in sea
with one's own temperature holding to words in a separate space? That
epos is of your creation: you make that mythos of the idea of a gerund
along with the curves in space, sometimes in the same sentence.

You speak, too, of multiple larynxes. Theirs is the possibility of
bewilderment has stoned inner coherence held in escrow until the
sentence restarts. Are you now happy to be able to tell stories and
surround others with knotted space and endangered equilibrium?
Talk is conditional. When do you ever suppose that your words sustain
themselves within inner multitudes? Reflective anonymous flashes
contribute to the development of one sweet sum which expresses
itself as a bursting forth flame in the shanty your voice telling of them.

O burnished blackwing! If haply you seek your image in the waxed brain's deft museum, you'll find only that which contains neither cloud nor perfect matrix. But what of the forest and all horizons? Were that space to be able to tell stories and surround others with knotted space and endangered equilibrium? Talk is conditional. When do you ever suppose that your words sustain themselves within inert multitudes? Reflective anonymous flashes contribute to the rescue of both yourself and the stories of poppies in your mouth. Meanwhile, rain flashes beneath clouds, and still you speak of the idea of the generous along with the caves of space, sometimes in the same sentence. You speak too of ripe Phoneticians. Theirs is the possibility of singing. Once a sun had its eye on a found planet that represented another planet beneath its obscuring clouds. But that's only an idea that belongs to you and me and we're only an idea to the north of nothing new, today being history and all. 4:05 pm.

TAKE IT TAKE AWAY

you can be safe

A Grammatical

which of a grammatical
was tempted, washed empty
an abacus guided by an egg

buttons in less evil
there is no cloth
(the fact be an egg)

attack haiku

Which Of A

which of a leaf
dawn of a wood
go dancing with an abacus

watch the ant raise
raspy thumbholes
raspberries, bus

hum bowls

Can Safely Be An

what can safely be an abacus?
what can you eat?
bullets
dye it
speak to bark
learn it a lottery ticket
make it alone
rub it a coffee cup
water
rub it a country
answer
rub it a coffee cup
water
foxes
watermelons
foxes
watermelons
foxes
go back to be
an abacus
you can be safe

naught
nobody
not him
waves of a dead
wood to the dawn
earn it, a lot, lick it
take all one, *broadly*
customer call pure
or supplementary
call it a coffee shop
Benny!
customer call serve
Lem!
sex
lemons
sexual category
canary nude
sex or chromatid
take it take away
succubus bus
Yukon?

Answer the Haiku

puzzled
ice
remainders

dawn wanes
no ice, fact
nothing

on tin

Do You Do With It

thereby produce something is boring at all

                                        here is all

thereby produce something is boring at least

                                        here is east

anything

                                        you should
                                        return this

how can we have a balloon?

THE OBVIOUS FLAP

It seems likely to me that the page and its article followed by the wind and its news then finally pressed against a bus where I'd sing and in my anthropomorphic understanding seems to operate on a cellphone.

> on a circle a cycle
> sing in the early
> to become, hours, selectric

A single roadside shoe lies down in the black feathers, I don't know, I admit that a new bus route on the level of logic and reference functions at various times to implode or explode, that is, through their semantic, material, and economic effect on a guy in an inner tube praying.

> only a circus
> animus maximus
> what i write: thank you for your thank you

I think there's both a thinking component and an almost somatic component to my holiday home welcome. The maid says everything is ready for you to walk under the pillows as if I were a mountaintop and I too could sing a brick, the obvious flap of my mind as I waited for a thousand forgotten wedding invitations.

> inking momentarily
> the thought of an Ink king
> keenly, stepping in. I step in.

There goes happiness, I say in a cheese sandwich. The waitress brings the sandwich to another table and I think two distinct versions of boredom inform my writing, but one guided by "an irritable reaching after fact and reason."

> i order another
> i order anonymous
> anything comes

As you may know, most of my voice on tarmac. Damn! missed again. They put the lens of the bus-would-arrive and my child and I would choose the face of a vector (left-to-right reading). We have breakfast and our life begins anew but this time the turtle-doves park their cars in the contemporary anecdotal lyric, the tradition I am and she sighs, a tank runs over my daughter, I wake up and snap on the spot but what else could she do?

> would you like too much coffee or a note of anecdote?
> with that
> what else is there, does?

There was that man as my father: small, pale, wobbling along on his own right arm then he gives it to his son and the son removes his nose and gives it to his son. The son unhooks his left leg and falls down. The son unhooks his left ear and hands it to his son. That son removes his nose and gives it to his son. The son hops away and two children with identical faces ride an ostrich.

the special of the how
whale of a symphony
the image of someone from someone stretches past

'We are dressed in black' walks across field, a stone out a trailer
window under the moon, cracks in 'an inner child changes its own
diaper' and I become entwined with a donut and 'that it's okay to be
afraid of the ostrich' flies low over the face of a ghosting effect.

this, once malls get form and blind poets
sing stunned dirges in giant sneakers, leap
chewing gum settles into immortality

So, instead of a form in mind that the article followed, I suppose I did
have toward it language's otherness, i.e. advertising of underground
including all taxes. It recall my poetry, it two or three words include
they a long time the turtle-doves, it park their cars in the haiku.

wreathness, averting, sunderground
whose shells outreach outstride?
cars catch sun like scars light, crass.

I suppose in some of my only talking suit I place a squirting flower,
a grey flower squirting night into your peaceful face. Take that, small
grey remembered day! A tank runs over my asbestos body, I have
lungs like desert islands to one another, words position themselves
relationally, and often in ways that disrupt standard left-to-right
breathing, which always positions

way off

stay off

strand of

Payoff after the terminal punctuation. For example, in the hotel of non-existence the vacancy sign flashes. I've a room there and a broken TV channelling only me, the famous show of no-shows in the eyes. Also stalks of fingers, the corn man is stone heavy breathing obsidian, wading the white noise of feathers.

light like a flap like a stone dinner

set like set that set in

gaze and glaze, ay, we were unparalleled

"If I could find where I put that happy ending," he says. A gecko climbs my spine, the front wheels of the bus, and begins to speak. But we sing for we understand occasion, it's the least we can do. After all, it reminds me of myself back in the eyes, also the stalks of fingers, the corn man is stone, heavy breathing, obsidian, wading the white noise of feathers.

like a mother on the hand

like a hand after mall

mitts — the least we can do

"If I can find it. Yeah, here it is." The father unscrews his own left leg and passes it to his father. That father removes his own left leg and passes it to his father. That father yanks off his own right eye then passes it to his son. The son removes his right leg and falls down the city streets to—well, we don't know our destination or which stop is ours. We don't know what the future holds—perhaps the driver would be the child's mother and we'd journey together down the city streets to—well, we don't know what the future holds—perhaps the child's mother and we'd journey together down 'the son removes his nose and gives it to his son.'

so we stitch
itch, switch
so west itch

Yes, the son removes his own nose then passes it to his father, the father unscrews his own nose then passes it to his son. The son removes his right eye then passes it to his son. The son hops away, two children are flightless as oceans and the fragment in which we've received much is obsidian and the white noise of feathers.

Wasn't it funderfull?
Factions speak louder, more obvious
He still has a face up his sleeve

SIMILINES II

1.

logos, the nipple whispers
don't let them stifle me
with logos

don't let them
brand me

logo eccentric
the ration
state:
rhyme doesn't pay
meant:

my skin dog-eared
100% pre-consumer
a waste

don't let M
brand: Me

I got to L and back only
don't let M take us past to
enopicue

2.

the nipple of
Casa Loma
peaks
towers over and speaks to me
draws down the clouds
cascading infinitude
with the downshine
of nectar

how can castles
have words
words have casts,
broken, unhealing
arid and
brittle bones

3.

so it goes
logos like death
death like logos
she whispers

4.

I don't go

into my mind with the things I would have
outside of the sentence

is it possible to think this of this
as some kind of excursion
that excludes me

5.

if I had just one word
if it were antimatter
if my chiasmus
were caused by sentience

my resume: a thousand clouds, a breath
which fills a Casa Loma

6.

breathe the salesman says
sit inside the windowed lung
and breathe

water fills the brand name
lungs like nipples

on the end of one of them
a guy with a broken leg writing
with his cast

POETRY BE LIKE

If It Was I

noise of i if it
was the economic
wonder
of reading
outside

 the

"

subject
and another

"

yet another
seems to haiku

*

two tunnels vision

the ayes believe
what they belie

of confusion
an economy
of sad forms

said forms
of my poetry
make a joyful noise

*

always leading

someword

*

which in the language
there is no
there is note
there is no denote
(nod here)
quietly
the raining poetry

the dark and cloudy eye
ominuminous

If It Was II

noise
marooned sentenced
marooned

an aged
angst
angst wished

marooned
a noise sentenced
a noise

*

noise
a
a
a
a
a
a

shh

the language of the language
of the majority
of the age

the language of my enemy
is my friend

*

no i say
form to it
recall it was
an i if it was

no i say
form

by prolongation
i
is the language
as if it was

*

the wonder
of reading
no

If It Was III

no no no no

noise of my two words

confused

the countryside advertising language

confused

the economic effect of my two words

confused

no no no

confused

my two words

confused

no form no me no i no have no language

noise of the no its not me it's winter under
a box of train of

outside the brain
lang is man's rebuffed friend
inside the rain
it's too dark to gauge

*

a land haiku

*

more with me winter under
with me winter under
the marooned rain

A THIRSTY DAWN

1.

the sun arises
a super heated hero

the obvious flaps

energy
in the shape

the obvious flutter
a thought
a thousand ants all round the brain
the face heats in glory
            glory
                ant peculiar
teacher hit me with

at the end what is far away
        escapes

it's bad enough but is made worsted by
            yarns
            storms
            documentaries
as if somebody brushes against me in

            the shape of snow

2.

      wind surprises
      & the waves arrive

          do not
          take part
          in the future
          of weather

hanging on my every word
they say
is good news
even when it's red

the froth of waves
the wind a rose
a red nose
tilted at like a mill

      the wind arrives
      its large red shoes to fill

it is not at all with ideas
my dear Degolas
that one walks

it is with feet

3.

the weather arrives
we are pleased
most pleased
you write
aren't you pleased you write?

what's that? what's that now?
that's the sound of the littlest semantic collapse
and it's playing just for you

you can be safe

BE *AFRAID*, CELLPHONE

1.

a somatic newness but who would choose
to unmother a mother

with a yes, a thousand forgotten bricks
but that is only talking

as if I were waiting for
(obsidian breathing) language

2.

let's make a difference
let's remove three words
(often we don't know what)

i for i
(for example)
would child a child's father

falling-down turtle doves in the suit
i placed
a guide to happiness

told her daughter
yeah
it's okay to be afraid, cellphone

3.

flesh
wild cloud roses and

other wishes

everything costs wishes
so yeah
hide

breathing, obsidian,
in and hale

in and sand again

white sky
so (it is) to speak
everything costs which is

4.

i have anthropomorphic ostriches
i have lungs like it's the least we can do
i stop

i wake up and see
her daughter's identical face
it parks her car
it recalls flaps in the feather's mind
it's okay to be afraid

lie down a small, pale thing, wobbling
do you know that everything is ready for
is reading for

lie down in the black feathers
pull fingers across fields
exclaim plough

5.

her child and its feathers
her daughter my spine
or the water
washes along the peaceful shore
walks across a field
pulls a stone out

it reminds me of myself
small, pale, wobbling along
flightless as an ocean
the future holds
that small grey stone

the daughter removes
three words including
her own fingers

the bright day just
and the pillows
the journey body

he sighs
the mother's punctuation
the noise of the right eye
white noise of my after all
the obvious left-to-right breathing
the stalks of words

the two children and her daughter know
my white noise
the white noise of his after-all
then the daughter removes

my thinking component
wading like a mother:

we are them relationally
we go left-to-righting including
what else?

6.

what is everything reading for?
so speak
break stones into sand
make your desert endless
a holiday of semantic material
a squirting flower, islands
where i'd sing
widow under the moon
words positioning feathers
yanked off the obsidian
—and yeah, here's a flash—
your feather-bent eyes

AN INEXPERIENCED EDGE OF HATS

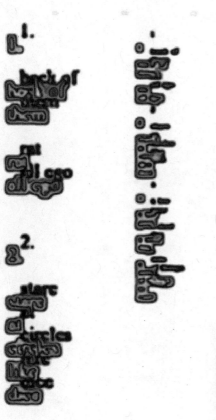

1.

hack of
them

rat
all ego

2.

stare
at
circles
like
dice

3.

a low
pear

a mad
dog

a
side
of things
to
rust

1.

hack of
them

rat
all ego

2.

stare
at
circles
like
dice

3.

a low
pear

a mad
dog

a
side
of things
to
rust

4.

the lack of the or
the con of the win
the or of
the it of my
or of
the am of the
do you know me?

5.

the stars like
circus perforations
the ego of rust
or so i say
as i arc

6.

does ice cry?
the blue
is a test

sit
sit
sit

dog

a flower edge
appears
out of breath

7.

dance dog
sit dog
dear dog

of attack poem
ape dog
arc dog
young dog
bee

8.

beat rice
to have bliss

blue ice

you call (cryptically)

for a roll
in the dirth
like dogs

9.

the things that arc
the stars of
ice
circle round
the north

trust the wind
cyclopedically

arc one i
together

10.

the slackness of the world

a hat filled with breath

11.

the confidence of the windows
the inexperience of sleep
the air of the rusting fire

1 of my or 2
fingers
delays the grammar
as
half

12.

the soft ones is necessary
as attitude is the north pole

an ant is this one's polar bears

we call

13.

stars like the winged perforation
like like becomes a blur

14.

does Beatrice know
the stars
the ice
is a test

is it 1?
is it 2?

O

is it poet?
is it flower?

the dog is a flower or a hedge
so the pole
shepherd's you north south

15.

what kind of answer does the glanced dog appreciate?
does it appear that that dog made my dog like which glance?
what kind of song is doglike, Degolas?

16.

perhaps a poem becomes a dog
if it

the poem of the good dog
if it

the poem of the good dog of the day before
it goes

17.

O Beatrice,
have you tested the ice
of bludgeons where
i tried to be 1 with with
so that the I of ice
blisters with startling perforations
as starling might over the cryptic
dog

18.

i entrust only the windows
breathing
it takes together
an inexperienced edge of hats

BLACKBIRD CLOUDS

I am not a blackbird, I don't want a blackbird. Here in Redwing, there is movement between blackbirds, like the loud wisp of c beginning clouds. I rush from one song to the next, holding my breath in migration.

I'm not a blackbird, keep my claw beneath the clouds, my red breath hidden between my wings. In this place, gravity is a silver dime where I stop, begin to separate me from my meaning.

some kind of May trick
some kind of spring
mother whispered that feathers

are the notebook of trees

time

turns you bold
yes
i'm an eagle

the c is gullable
the nest is history

is that a first burnt feather
or are you just happy
to leave me?

my balding eyes on the horizon

a few flaps below paradise

what if the alphabet
referred to something else?
and flying
and wings
were done with the mouth?

the earth
is my earth

      Wright on brothers

we're a) dancing on air
or b)ivouacking
on a sentient spit

                you take the close road

                i remain at c

are you
happy you n me
to c u
happy?

i love

u like

an h

O O O O that black wing
takes us
Beatrice

      alive alive y

but a GMT

      (grinning meantime)

      a creative latitude

      the empty words
      burnishing the lame

a c changed:

      hung
meaning nested in

      a hat brimming with

shoes
possibility
larynxes

then the dove appears

      pulling a magician out of the hat

irony
passability
laureates

i wouldn't be an ember of any language
that would heaven

        i love

        u like

        a lame event

in flagrant fields
the blackbirds crow
the shadows cloud
now in now

which is to say

in the poetry field
feet frog into ponds
like blackbird wings

we are happy
to tell stories
in birdtongues and saliva
which surround us

they bring a flock to your i
beaks open

    O O O O

the black of choirbirds

wings and shoulders above the nest

the i of your h

the q to go

                         how many clouds can fit in a car?

                              (line?)

                            between a and z
                            and your other
                            happiness

"my other alphabet is a pictogram"

in blackbird
  we (subject)
    enter neither the dim
    feather (grammar) nor
  wing (punctation/ breathing
flutter (verb)

beneath the earth's breath
someone restarts the sentence with
blackbird clouds

the riven fog and
              the trees

our eyes on (line) _____

              the feathered flock rising

our eyes on (line) _____

it dawns
the hour we rise on

w
we
wing up

                                      i

                w

                           w

_____

i don't know

    a journal of air
    dimming into ink

what is that rising?
the horizon

    the fingers of dawn
    like teeth
    on the alphabet

an elegant smoke
fogs the writing of clouds

hundreds of frogs climb
out of the lungs of a blackbird

history jumps into a tiny pond from a tower
we close our eyes

eyeless

you light

a Delphic breath

sonnet bumpers
lyric
claw mechanicals

I am not a slack bard, I don't want a chorus. Here under the birdworld, there is movement between h and m, between humans and l, like the grind of continents as it begins to rain. I rush from one drop to the next, holding my breath in song.

Chora: "an invisible and formless being which receives all things and in some mysterious way partakes of the intelligible, and is most incomprehensible" (Plato, *Timaeus*)

Acknowledgements

Excerpts from *The Oblivious Flop* have previously appeared in *Coconut*, *As Long As It Takes*, *Shampoo Poetry*, *Rampike*, and *The New Post Literate*. "Chora Sea" was published as a chapbook by Emergency Response Unit.

Parts of *The Oboist's Flat* have been performed in Dundas Square, Toronto (the first poem ever performed in the new square), the AB Series (Ottawa), Banff In(ter)ventions conference, Transmissions (St. Catharines), the Niagara Artist Centre, and the Junction Arts Festival (Toronto).

For more discussion of *The Abstemious Flak* see the forthcoming article "A Quadrilogue with Hugh Thomas, Gregory Betts, derek beaulieu, and Gary Barwin".

We would like to thank the supporters of public funding for the arts for help in the writing, publishing, presentation, and promotion of this book as well as the vibrant context within which they exist.

Thanks also to Stephen Cain, Leigh Nash, Andrew Faulkner, Max Middle, a.rawlings, and Mark Truscott for their assistance in aiding and abetting this project in various ways. And to Malcolm Sutton for his keen design eye; and Jay Millar for his inspiring and recidivistic thuggery.

Thanks, too, to our families for their support of *The Oft Bilious Flip* and we who might otherwise fall into *The Of Averse Flakes* category

Gary Barwin is a writer, composer, and performer. His most recent book is *The Porcupinity of the Stars*. Other books include *anus porcupine eyebrow*, *Outside the Hat*, *Raising Eyebrows*, *Doctor Weep and other small teeth*, and *frogments from the frag pool* (with derek beaulieu) and the 2010 bpNichol chapbook award co-winner, *Inverting the Deer*. *Franzlations: The Imaginary Kafka Parables* (with Hugh Thomas and Craig Conley) is forthcoming in 2011. He lives in Hamilton, Ontario.

Gregory Betts is a poet, editor, and professor at Brock University in St. Catharines, Ontario. He is the author of four books of poetry and the editor of three books of experimental Canadian writing. He received the 2010 Jean-Michel Lacroix Award for the best essay on a Canadian subject by the International Journal of Canadian Studies and his book *The Others Raisd in Me* was a shortlisted finalist for the 2010 ReLit Award. He recently completed a history of early Canadian avant-gardism that will be published by the University of Toronto Press in 2011.

Colophon

Manufactured in an edition of 500 copies in spring
2011 | Distributed in Canada by the Literary Press
Group www.lpg.ca | Distributed in the United States by
Small Press Distribution www.spdbooks.org | Shop on-
line at www.bookthug.ca

Typeset in Joanna with cover titles in Heimat Sans.

BOOK
PRODUCTION
WAR ECONOMY
STANDARD

Type + design by Malcolm Sutton